J394.264

W9-BJU-195

DELPHI PUBLIC LIBRARY

222 East Main Street
Delphi, Indiana 46923
765-564-2929

J394, 264

Sarah
Gives Thanks

MIKE ALLEGRA

illustrated by
DAVID GARDNER

Albert Whitman & Company
Chicago, Illinois

Library of Congress Cataloging-in-Publication Data

Allegra, Mike.
Sarah gives thanks : how Thanksgiving became a national
holiday / by Mike Allegra ; illustrated by David Gardner.
p. cm.
ISBN 978-0-8075-7239-9 (hardcover)
1. Thanksgiving Day—History—Juvenile literature.
2. Hale, Sarah Josepha
Buell, 1788-1879—Juvenile literature.
I. Gardner, David, ill. II. Title.
GT4975.A48 2012
394.2649—dc23
2011034161

Text copyright © 2012 by Mike Allegra.
Illustrations copyright © 2012 by David Gardner.
Published in 2012 by Albert Whitman & Company.
All rights reserved. No part of this book may be
reproduced or transmitted in any form or by any means,
electronic or mechanical, including photocopying,
recording, or by any information storage and retrieval
system, without permission in writing from the publisher.
Printed in China.
10 9 8 7 6 5 4 3 2 1 BP 16 15 14 13 12

The design is by Nick Tiemersma.

For more information about Albert Whitman & Company,
please visit our Web site at www.albertwhitman.com.

To Ellen. — M.A.

For Mark, with all my love — and endless thanks. — D.G.

The turkey was fresh from the oven. Sarah Josepha Hale asked her five children to join hands in thanksgiving.

The baby grabbed on to Sarah's finger, but the other four hesitated. Sarah understood. They had just returned from their father's grave and were not in a thankful mood.

So she bowed her head alone.

"Dear Lord, we are thankful for having known him," she began. "We are thankful for his love. And we are thankful for the love we have for each other."

As Sarah spoke, her children fumbled for each other's hands. As one, they thanked God for their good fortune.

After she said "Amen," Sarah sent out one last silent prayer: "Please, God, help me find a way to support my family."

Sarah knew she needed to find a job to raise five children. Did good jobs for women even exist? She couldn't think of a single one.

It wouldn't be easy, but Sarah vowed to find a way.

Selling hats was not the way. It wasn't long before Sarah couldn't stand the sight of those feathered and flowered, gaudy and garish, *completely useless* hats.

But it wasn't all bad. When no customers were to be found, she reached for her pen and wrote.

Sarah always loved to write.

Sarah's love for words began when she was a young girl. Her mother, Martha Buell, taught her the books of the Bible, the plays of Shakespeare, and the poetry of Milton. Sarah soon wanted to know more. Much more.

But to Sarah's great disappointment, women weren't allowed to go to college. A woman was expected to be a housewife and mother. She didn't need a college education to do those things.

After her older brother, Horatio, was admitted to Dartmouth College, however, Sarah saw her chance. When he was home on breaks, she burrowed into his textbooks and peppered him with questions.

Horatio didn't want to think about school on his summer vacation, but Sarah insisted.

"I am not going to go away, Horatio," she told him. "Therefore you might as well do as I ask."

Horatio knew this was true.

So Sarah received a college education without ever going to college.

Sarah's education continued after she married David Hale, a lawyer, in 1813. They loved each other and they both loved words. Each evening in their cozy New Hampshire home after putting the children to bed, they would perch in front of the fire and read and talk into the night.

David admired his wife's writing and encouraged her to submit her poetry to magazines. A few of Sarah's pieces were published. She liked seeing her work in print.

Then David died in 1822 and everything changed.

Sarah was so filled with grief, she insisted on wearing a black dress every day for the rest of her life.

Whenever Sarah found a spare moment, she wrote. But this time, it wasn't for the thrill of seeing her work in print—it was to keep her family from starving.

Soon, Boston magazines began to feature Sarah's writing. Much to Sarah's delight, with many publications came *payment*. Now, after putting the children to bed, she would perch in front of the fire with a pen and pot of ink and work into the night, scratching out words to put food on her table.

The Hale's Thanksgiving of 1826 was quite different from the one of four years earlier. Sarah wasn't earning much as an author, but the family's fortunes were improving. Magazines continued to print her work. Her book of poetry, *The Genius of Oblivion*, sold well. Her children were well fed and happy and receiving good educations.

The prayer of thanks before dinner was especially long.

Late that evening, Sarah resumed work on her first novel, *Northwood*. She riffled through the pages and found the exact spot for some thoughts that had been rattling around her brain all day:

We have too few holidays. Thanksgiving, like the Fourth of July, should be considered a national festival and observed by all our people.

Thanksgiving was not celebrated by everyone in the 1820s. Different states observed the holiday on different days. In the Southern states, Thanksgiving was usually not celebrated at all. The Pilgrims settled in Massachusetts, so many considered it a New England holiday.

But, to Sarah, Thanksgiving was not about the Pilgrims and the Indians and their famous feast. Thanksgiving was about what that feast *meant*. The holiday helped Sarah to look beyond her personal problems and appreciate what she had.

That message could be of value to everyone, she thought, from North to South and everywhere in between.

Northwood was published in 1827. It was a success.

The book soon led to a job offer. The publisher of a new women's magazine thought Sarah would be a great editor.

"Editress," she insisted.

So be it.

With the promise of steady work, Sarah Hale packed up her family and headed to Boston.

There were a number of women's magazines in Boston. They were all edited by men, and they devoted page after page to English and French fashions (and their horrible hats!).

Sarah made sure *Ladies' Magazine* was different. She printed articles on history and science and new schools for women. And she urged women to exercise—even though, at the time, women who did so were called the ultimate naughty word: *unladylike*.

The magazine thrived, and in 1837, Sarah went on to become the editress of another, larger magazine. Before long, she turned *Lady's Book* into the most widely read magazine in the country.

Sarah Josepha Hale became a household name. People listened to her. If she gave a book a good review, it turned into a best-seller. If she encouraged people to donate to a charity or a patriotic cause, the money came pouring in. Her opinions mattered.

And her opinion about Thanksgiving never changed.

Each fall, Sarah wrote about Thanksgiving in her magazine. She explained how it promoted family, friendship, gratitude, and religion. She even offered a delicious recipe for pumpkin pie.

With each passing year, more and more families across America celebrated the holiday.

She also dashed off letters to governors, businessmen, diplomats, and admirals, asking for their support for a national Thanksgiving holiday to be held on the last Thursday of November.

Those who didn't pledge their support often lived to regret it. In 1852, Sarah wrote:

Last year 29 States and all the Territories united in the festival. This year, we trust that Virginia and Vermont will come into this arrangement.

Women across the country read Sarah's editorial. All of them learned that the governors of Virginia and Vermont were *not* among Thanksgiving's supporters—and wasn't that a shame?

Letters of complaint arrived by the sackful.

Governors listened to the popular editress, but only the president could make Thanksgiving a national holiday.

Beginning in 1849, Sarah made an annual tradition of making her case to the president. Unfortunately, the president made an annual tradition of ignoring her.

PRESIDENT
ZACHARY TAYLOR

PRESIDENT
MILLARD FILLMORE

She wrote letters to President Zachary Taylor. Then to Millard Fillmore. Then to Franklin Pierce. Then to James Buchanan. None of them listened.

"I am not going to go away," Sarah said. "Therefore the president might as well do as I ask."

The next president was Abraham Lincoln.

When Lincoln received Sarah's letter, the nation was in the middle of the Civil War. Lincoln understood that sometimes it was hard to remember good things in bad times. People needed a day to be thankful for food on their tables, roofs over their heads, and the blessings in their lives.

Thanksgiving was exactly what this nation needed.
President Lincoln did as Sarah asked.

On October 3, 1863, Lincoln issued a proclamation declaring a national day of thanksgiving. It would be held on the last Thursday of November. The holiday has been celebrated every year since.

Sarah Hale's dream of a unified, national Thanksgiving had finally come true. It took her thirty-six years, but she didn't mind.